Dos Chiles

Two Chilies

DOS CHILES / TWO CHILIES
ISBN: 978-0-9839575-0-8

An Inlandia Institute Publication
Riverside, California

Copyright © 2012 by Julianna Maya Cruz
All rights reserved
Published by the Inlandia Institute

Cover design by Julie Frenznick
Book layout by Cati Porter

This book, while based on actual persons and events, contains fictional elements and therefore should be considered a work of fiction.

No part of this book may be reproduced, stored in a retrieval system, or transmitted in any form or by any means, electronic, mechanical, photocopying, recording, or otherwise, without written permission of the author. For information about adopting this publication for classroom use or regarding permissions, please write to:
Inlandia Institute
4178 Chestnut Street
Riverside, CA 92501

Printed in the U.S.A.
This edition first printing, April 2012

Dos Chiles

Two Chilies

Julianna Maya Cruz

An Inlandia Institute Publication
Riverside, California

Dedicated to all those who add to the olla—
Muchísimas Gracias

Contents

1: Chili is Home	1
2: Mix in Every Ingredient with Love	12
3: Time Helps the Flavors Develop	22
4: Riverside, Oranges, Roses, & Magdalena	28
5: Always Make Chili with Someone You Love	34
Nuñez Family Green Chili Recipe	41
Epilogue	43
Glossary	45
Nuñez Family Album	47
About the Author	45

1

Chili is Home

Nothing else can make your mouth water like the savory aroma of New Mexico Green Chile, *frijoles*, and fresh homemade *tortillas*. The smell of fire-roasted chiles meets you from around the corner and down the street. It summons you and commands that you return home. You have no choice but to follow the scent trail left by the desert zephyr that blew through your hair and wrapped itself around you. When you walk in the door, a second layer of flavor greets you—frijoles— rich and earthy.

Your stomach starts to growl and your other senses kick in. You hear the slap, slap, roll, slap, roll of the perfectly circular tortillas being made on the same board that has been worn in and perfectly seasoned by so many years of love. As you stand there, hypnotized for a moment, you realize you are home. Home is where my story begins.

"Grandpa, you are cleaning chilies without me? When are you going to teach me how to make your chili?" I asked. "And, you said that you would help me with my 6th grade Social Studies project."

"Well, maybe we can do both." Grandpa smiled his sly smile that let me know he was up to something good.

"Right now? But how are you going to tell me about why our family came to Riverside and make chili at the same time?"

"That's easy. Making really good chile is a lot like telling a good story. All the ingredients have their own place and purpose—just like the events in life that lead to where you are now."

"Okay, so then what's first?" I tried to read the wrinkles on Grandpa's face, but had no idea what he was about to tell me.

"Patience."

"*What?* But I thought you said you would teach me *now?*"

"I am. Patience is the first ingredient in making good chile. It's also one of the first lessons I learned when I was little. Helping my dad in the garden is one of my earliest mem... "

"I *love* gardening!" I interrupted. "My favorite vegetables to grow are *calabasitas*. They get big so fast! Oh, and *pepinos*! They taste so sweet and they cool your mouth off when the chili is too hot—I love gardening!" I jabbered on.

"You are so eager to learn, Julianna! But you must learn to slow down and listen. Let me finish my story."

"Oh, sorry Grandpa. I just got excited."

"Okay then, I must have been about four years old. I thought I was doing such a good job helping because I had picked a whole bush worth of chiles. When I showed them to my dad, he just shook his head with disappointment. He told me that the best chiles must be left on the plant a little longer. Don't pick them when they are too young. They need to go through some suffering before they are spicy enough. It's kind of like they are earning their flavor by surviving the dry, hot summer days. So, you must learn to wait."

"Oh, trust me, I learned the hard way that the nice little plump ones are not as hot as the older sunburnt ones! Remember that chili eating dare I had with Uncle Juan?"

"Just like your Mama—so stubborn and ready for a challenge." Grandpa interrupted me this time.

"Anyway, he tried to be nice and offered me the little plump one, but I didn't trust him and I took the older scarred one. That was the hottest chili I ever ate! My tongue felt like it was on fire and I could feel that chili burning all the way down to my stomach! Well, that will help me remember patience—let the chili suffer a little."

Grandpa raised his bushy left eyebrow and gave me that look. You know, that look that grown-ups give that says, *"yeah right."* "Okay, well I don't think you've learned patience yet, but at least you've learned which chiles will have the most flavor. Let's go start the fire so we can roast these chiles."

We walked outside to the patio to start the fire and Grandpa started splitting wood into skinny shivers so that they would catch on fire quickly. I loved being outside. Just then, the smell in the air reminded me of camping—I loved camping—especially in the mountains. The sharp smack of the axe splitting the wood snapped me back to reality.

"Grandpa, can I try to cut the wood?" I wanted so much to be able to use Grandpa's axe. I knew it was the same axe he used when he was my age, and I longed to hold the smooth wood in my hand.

Grandpa looked back at the house as though he was checking to make sure no one was watching and he handed me the axe.

"I suppose you are old enough…I remember having to cut shivers of wood to start the fire every morning before the sun came up. And I was younger than you are now."

"Why did you have to make a fire every day?" I held the axe in my hand and it felt so warm and powerful. The axe was so sharp it went through the wood like a warm knife cutting through butter. I was so happy that I finally got to prove to Grandpa I could do it. I made a neat little pile of shivers and Grandpa smiled his proud smile as he went on with the story.

"Well, when I was about ten years old we moved from Kelly, New Mexico to Magdalena. My grandparents, your great grandparents, had a ranch there and I learned how to be a rancher. Our house was a tiny adobe, and it had a little wood stove inside that was for cooking and keeping warm. So If I didn't cut and bring in wood, I wouldn't get breakfast. And I needed all the food I could get because we had so many chores!"

"More than me? I have to clean my room and the bathroom every day after school."

"Way more. Life on the *rancho* was hard. Every morning I had to chop the wood for the fire and feed the chickens before school. Then I had to ride the bus to school—for three hours! Can you imagine?"

I started carefully leaning the shivers onto each other like a tent, and tore up some newspaper to put inside it. I had watched Grandpa make a fire this way many times, and I knew it would start right up. Then he could add the bigger pieces after the little ones were burning hot enough. Grandpa stopped his story, and watched me to make sure I did it right. When I realized he stopped talking, I tried to keep the story going.

"Three hours? That's longer than our field trip to Mission San Juan Capistrano!"

"Yes. Then after school we had more chores. I would ride the range with my dad. We would make sure the livestock had enough water, fix fences, and sometimes we had to move the whole herd from one area to another because they had eaten everything."

"That sounds like fun! I'd much rather do *that* than the chores I have to do." I was imagining riding the range and what it would feel like to be out there working hard, but never getting bored.

"Well, you just think it's fun because you don't have to do it. It was a lot of hard work and we had to do it even when it was really hot and dry or in the freezing rain—sometimes even in the snow. Some days, I wished I didn't have to go. But then the relief of spring time would come. After the rains, the desert smelled of sweet sage and mesquite, and wet earth. My reward was knowing that I had learned to work hard, and that my family could depend on me."

"So, were you kind of like a little chili? Having to suffer so that you could be your best?"

"Ha, ha...yes and now look at me...I'm a spicy old grandpa!" Just then, I could see every wrinkle on Grandpa's face and the scars on his hands—he *did* look like a chili that had seen its share of hot summer days.

We both laughed and he handed me the box of wooden matches to light the fire. The heat from the flames radiated up, and it made my eyes water as we put the grate over the fire pit. I could smell the burnt chunks of chilies past reigniting with the new flames. It reminded me that it had been too long since the last time we made chili, and I eagerly placed the bright green chilies on the grill. They sizzled and popped as their skin started to blister. The smell brought back so many memories—every fall we had to roast the big bags of chilies that Uncle Julian brought back from New Mexico, so we'd have enough for the winter because Christmas isn't merry without green chili. While we watched over the chilies, turning them every now and then, Grandpa reminded me that we needed to finish what we started. I looked at my Grandpa with eyes of wonder—I wondered how he got all those wrinkles. Were they from smiling in the wind? Or were they from squinting in the sun on hot desert days? I wondered about all those grey hairs—did he worry too much about my mama, brother, and me?

Like most twelve year olds, my mind wandered easily, and I was imagining what it would be like to ride a horse every day. Then I started thinking about what it would have been like to spend so much time with my Dad. My only memory of Dad was of him bringing green Jello from his catering truck to make me smile when I had the mumps—why can't I remember anything else? I wondered why he left. Did I do something to make him mad? How could he just leave us like that? He didn't even say "Good-bye"— nothing. I was feeling mad and sad all at once, but I didn't want to feel that, so I just tried to push it away. I got back to horses. A horse wouldn't just leave you.

"I wish I had a horse—you must have loved having a horse—wasn't it fun to ride all the time?"

"Well, I learned a very valuable lesson from my horse once. You keep watch on these chiles and I'll tell you the story."

"Okay, is this your way of teaching me to work hard? It's hot over here!"

"Yes—you need to suffer a little" Grandpa said with a sly smile. "On to my story—One day when I was about fifteen years old, I was mounting one of our horses and he started to buck. The next thing I knew, I landed so hard on the ground that all the wind got knocked out of me. I was so scared that I didn't even want to get up. I could feel the tears starting to come to the edge of my eyes, but I didn't want my dad to see me cry. Heck, at fifteen I didn't want *anyone* to see me cry. So I just sat there on the dusty ground. When I finally had the nerve to look up, I saw my dad there. He was looking at me with his serious look and said, 'Either you get up on that horse or I'll sell it *and* your saddle—being that you won't have any use for either.' Well guess what, I got back up on that horse in a hurry! Lesson learned, "Don't let setbacks in life intimidate you—face your fears head-on!" I knew Grandpa was serious about facing fears because he had his fists clenched like he was ready to fight.

"Oh, Grandpa—I know that must have hurt, but that sort of reminds me of learning to ride my bike. Every time I fell you said, 'Well, do we need to sell your bike? Or are you going to get back on it and try again?' I remember thinking that was kind of mean, but you were just trying to teach me a lesson. I get it Grandpa, and I did finally learn to ride my bike because I didn't quit."

"That's right, M'hunny. Now back to the chiles. They smell like they're done."

Grandpa inspected my work and with a nod of approval started taking them off of the grill and putting them in a big ceramic bowl that was painted with flowers and Saguaro cactus on the side. "Here, you put the lid tight. We want them to sweat so they will be easy to peel."

"Why is it that everything worth anything always comes from sweating?" I picked up the bowl and could feel the heat of the chilies come right through. "These are gonna be really good Grandpa."

2

Mix in Every Ingredient with Love

While letting the chilies cool a bit, we chopped the garlic, onions, and tomatoes. We sliced the meat into nice square cubes that looked like the dice we used at school to practice math. That reminded me that I wasn't finished getting all of Grandpa's story for my Social Studies project. I still needed to find out why he decided to move our family from New Mexico to California. So, I thought I'd sneak some questions in while we worked.

"So, what's next Grandpa? What else can you tell me about why you moved out to California?"

"Well, next you need to peel those chiles. Remember, don't touch your eyes, and don't forget to rinse the seeds out or the chili will be too hot."

"Mom says I should use gloves for this part."

"Well, we didn't have gloves in the old days." said Grandpa. "If our hands burned too much, we just soaked them in milk—*after* we finished making the chile."

"Oh, I get it—I need to suffer a little—is that it?" I mumbled, but the look on Grandpa's face let me know that I should stop being a smart-alec and get to work.

"So do you want to hear more of my story, or not?" he asked.

"Of course, you haven't even gotten to when you're grown up yet."

"Okay, so when you're done peeling the chiles, chop them on this cutting board and I'll start mixing our ingredients together while I tell you the next part of my story."

Grandpa put the big cast iron pot on the stove and let it get good and hot. I always thought of that pot as magic, because all you had to do was heat it and it started to smell like chili—even with nothing in it! Next, he added oil and the little cubes of meat. When they started to ooze their juices a little, he sprinkled on the flour. This made nice tasty brown bits of goodness on the bottom of the pot. When the meat was done browning, and was perfectly crisped on all sides, he scooped the meat out of the pan and let it rest in a bowl. Then he added the onions and gave them a stir. When the onions got clear, he added in the garlic and tomatoes while I added in my chilies.

He gave that a stir, mixing the flavors together. To this heavenly aroma, he added the broth and told me to scrape all the little brown crispies off of the bottom. Finally, he added the meat back into the pot. My mouth was watering. My stomach was growling. And I had forgotten all about my burning hands.

"Grandpa, you did all that so fast and you forgot to tell me your story."

"Oops, sometimes I just get caught up. Ok, so on to the 'grown -up' part of the story. You put the lid on and listen. When I was about twenty years old, I joined the Civilian Conservation Corps (or CCC). Back then, times were tough for everyone. It was The Great Depression, and work was hard to find. Being the oldest boy, I had to help the family. So, I joined the CCC and was promised $30.00 dollars a month. My job was to help build roads, fix railroads, dig wells and water ways. It was very hard work, but it made a man out of me—and not too soon. After I was discharged from the CCC, I came home to find out that my dad had been very sick. He died soon after. That left me as the 'Man of the House.' My mother, and my younger sisters and brother were depending on me for everything.

"Oh, Grandpa, that's so sad." I looked up at him with tears in my eyes.

"Don't cry, *Mija*. Remember, every event--even the sad ones--are what bring you to where you are now. Just like adding all your ingredients into the pot makes your chile taste great. You don't leave out the onion because it makes you cry when you cut it, and you don't leave out the chiles because they make your hands burn when you peel them. It's all important and has its purpose."

"Okay, keep going then." I said as I carefully wiped the tears away using my shirt sleeve so the burn of the chilies wouldn't get into my eyes.

"Well, for the next few years, I found work wherever I could," continued Grandpa. "Sometimes I worked in the silver mines in Kelly. Sometimes I would help herd the cattle onto the railroad cars in Magdalena. I traveled all the way to Las Cruces to find odd jobs—I even fixed people's fences. Then I heard about a government job farming in Arizona. So I went out there to work and sent the money back home. We did everything on those farms from plowing to harvesting—all kinds of foods and even stuff like cotton."

"Did you just keep working like that until you met my Grandma?"

"Well now, don't rush me. Let me tell you what happened to me when I was about 23. I got a very important letter—from the government. Along with a lot of other guys, I was drafted into the Army. That was 1943, and they sent me to Texas, then to California, and then on to the South Pacific. Talk about facing my fears—I didn't really even know how to swim and there I was surrounded by water. It was a very scary time, and I learned that war is a horrible thing—but we were told that we needed to defend our country—so we did. And finally, I got to come back home in 1946."

"Oh my gosh, Grandpa—that was three years! I hope I never have to fight in a war!"

"I know—I hope you don't have to, either. I spent three years trying to believe that if I was at war somewhere far away, then my family was safer. But I don't like to think about wars. I like to remember 1946 as the best year of my life. That's when I met your Grandma; it was 'love at first sight.'"

"Aw, this sounds like the happy part of your story." I checked the chili and gave it a stir. The earthy roasted aroma leaked out from under the lid and filled the room. Both Grandpa and I took a deep breath to let the chili fill us up. "Okay on to the good stuff, Grandpa."

"Yes, on to the good stuff. It was 1946 and Juan and I were sitting at a USO dance when we saw these two really pretty ladies sitting on the other side of the room. Juan gave me a sly smile and a nod. Then we got up the courage to go over there and ask them to dance. Well, it turned out they were sisters! We really hit it off and well, you know the rest—by August of that year, I married Martha Chavez (your Grandma to be). And Juan married your Great-Aunt Beatrice; they were the best dance partners—they even won Jitter Bug contests!"

"Jitter Bug?! What kind of dance is that? Is it like the Funky Chicken, or the Macarena?"

"Well, they did a lot of jumping around. Kind of like a bug with burning feet dancing across the hot desert floor."

Grandpa danced his fingers wildly across the palm of his hand to show me what it looked like, and we both giggled.

"And what about you and Grandma, did you dance the Jitter Bug too?"

"Yes. But we didn't get as crazy as Juan and Bea." Grandpa smiled like he was enjoying that memory.

"So what happened next?"

"A lot happened during those years. Your Grandma and I made many batches of chile together. We learned to combine the ingredients in just the right way until we made our perfect pot of chile. On July 18, 1947, your mama was born. I became a daddy! Your Grandma and I were very proud parents. We named your mama Magdalena, after the "Lady of the Mountain." Mary Magdalene watches over the little town of Magdalena—you can see her in curves of the mountains. We were so happy, but I knew it took more than happiness to feed a family and we couldn't make it on what little I could earn working part-time while going to the university on the G.I. Bill."

"Well what made you decide to go to California?" I threw my hands up like Mama always did when she didn't understand why I did something. "I mean, you didn't even know anybody, right?" I shook my head like I thought he was crazy for leaving New Mexico just when things were getting good.

"I really liked California when the Army sent me there for training. The weather was always nice and there was so much to do. You have to understand, California was the 'Land of Opportunity' to most young men. But, like any other move it was a big risk. We didn't have much money, and like you said, no family to turn to. Everyone was trying to talk us out of leaving. I have to admit, I was scared. Let's just say a lot of thinking and worrying went into that decision. Finally, we decided to just go. We wanted to give our kids more opportunities than we had. We had to put fear aside and just do it."

"What did you do to find a job? And what about a place to live?"

"We did have a little money saved up. Plus we brought as much food as we could carry. We drove out in an old Chevy and took Route 66 the whole way. When we finally got to California, we just stayed in a motel that had a little kitchen in the room. I started looking for work right away. After a few months of doing odd-jobs to survive, I finally got a job at North American Aviation. Luckily, my timing was good and California's aviation industry was growing. They were looking for people with military experience. So, it was my experience in the Army, my great math skills, and the classes I took at the University of New Mexico that helped me get that job. I was earning enough money to rent an apartment, and by 1949, we were living pretty comfortably in the Servicemen's Projects in Los Angeles. That's the year your Uncle Julian was born."

"Didn't you miss all the family back home?"

"Of course, but California had so much to offer and your Grandma really loved going to the beach. The Pike, in Long Beach, was our favorite place—the sound of the roller coaster, the salty air, and the sweet, chewy taffy. Your Mama loved the taffy. It was just a quick drive along Highway 1 to get there. Once we had a house, we invited your Great Aunt Bea and Uncle Juan to come visit. They would come out whenever they could, and we would go back to Magdalena whenever we could. Bea and Juan really loved the salty beach air and we would take them to the beach whenever they came to visit. Bea would put sand in a little jar and take it out when it was too hot in Magdalena. She would smell the salty sand, and imagine herself at the beach."

"Well, it sounds like you made it. And it smells like the chili is really coming together. Can I try some?"

"Not yet. My story is not done, so the chile can't possibly be done." Grandpa reminded me to be patient.

3

Time Helps the Flavors Develop

Grandpa continued his story about life in California, but sometimes he would stop and I could tell he was thinking about what he should tell me and what he shouldn't. I wanted so much to just scream, "Tell me everything!" But I knew that wouldn't work. I had read in our Social Studies book about all the hard times that Hispanics had in California. So, I knew it couldn't have been all "fresh air and sandy beaches." I guess Grandpa didn't want me to feel sorry for him or something.

"Okay, Grandpa. I'm not that little anymore. Just tell me, wasn't it hard moving out here?" I wondered if he had to learn to ignore people sneering at him, and calling him names like I had seen in the *Zoot Suit* movie. I thought about my Mama's story of the Nuns undoing her pretty braids to check for lice—just because they thought she was a dirty Mexican. I hate people like that!

"Of course it was hard—everything is hard at first. But just like making chile—you learn what to do and what *not* to do. And after a while, you stop acting like you're the new guy. You start saying to yourself, 'Hey, this is *my* home. And at home, I work hard so my family can depend on me.' There's no time or place for complaining, Míja. So, if I tell you all the little things that I didn't like, all I would be doing is complaining, and what do you ever get from that? It doesn't change anything. When your hands burn from peeling chiles does crying about it make your hands feel better? No, you must *do* something about it."

"I know. You soak your hands in milk, right?" I added to show him that I understood.

"Yes. And don't forget you have to give things time. For the chile, time helps the flavors develop. All the ingredients have time to tell their own story and blend together with the others. Whenever you are trying something new, do you get it right off? Well, maybe you do sometimes, but most times you need to develop the skills over time. So, with time and hard work, we turned California into our home by blending our ingredients with the others around us."

I thought for a while about that *blending*. Is that what they meant when they called America the "Great Melting Pot?" The only problem I had with that was it meant my Grandpa (really, our whole family) gave up some things to be more like the other ingredients in the pot. To be part of the soup in the melting pot, we gave up speaking Spanish—that kind of made me angry. I wanted to be able to speak Spanish like my Grandma and Grandpa. I could understand them, but I couldn't just speak it like they did because they never spoke in Spanish to me. Spanish was always like their secret code—if they didn't want me to hear something, they would say it in Spanish. Little did they know, I'm a quick learner. Plus, they always let little words leak out when they couldn't remember how to say them in English. Then I started thinking that I shouldn't be complaining, and I certainly wasn't going to complain to Grandpa. I guess if I was going to learn to speak Spanish, I was going to have to do it myself. I thought it was weird the way my aunts and uncle didn't even want to learn Spanish. I wondered if my Grandpa had told them not to so they could "fit in" better. My mom, on the other hand, was the rebel. When she went back to school at Riverside

Community College, and later at UCR, she met a lot of other friends that were all about the Chicano Movement and then she felt proud to know Spanish. She felt proud to be herself. But I was spending most of my time with Grandma and Grandpa so I didn't really get to be part of that. Again, I realized that my mind had wandered—back to it! Get the whole story!

"Okay, so we're not even close to being done with this story Grandpa. What about when my uncle and aunts were born? What were you doing then? Were you living in the Pine Street house yet?" I wanted to make sure he finished before we got sidetracked.

"Yes, yes! By 1956 your Uncle Julian, your Aunt Luella, and your Aunt Beatrice were all born and we were living in the house on Pine Street in Lynwood. I loved that little house. It was on a nice quiet street with trees and sidewalks. We even had a front porch and a big back yard. Do you remember?"

"Oh yes! My favorite thing was climbing up into the apricot tree and tossing the sweet ripe ones down to Grandma. We would sit in the shade under the tree and eat them. Sometimes we ate so many, we didn't even take any back to the house." I smiled remembering those fun times. "And I remember

Grandma washing my hair *with vinegar* in the big kitchen sink—she said it made my hair shiny, but I didn't like the smell, so she gave some of her lilac perfume to put under my nose. You know, sometimes when the breeze is just right outside, I smell that perfume and there aren't even any lilac bushes in the yard! Weird, *¿qué no?*"

"No. Not weird *Míja*—it's just Grandma." And with that I saw a little tear in Grandpa's eye. So I tried to change the subject. "Well, what about me? How old were you when I was born?"

"Well, I guess we'll have to skip some years, but that's kind of how it goes anyway—the years just fly by. I turned around and I was almost 45—and *you* were born. Oh my gosh! I was a Grandpa! I couldn't believe it! Everybody wanted to hold you—especially your Grandma. She made sure your Mama learned all about being a mother. You even had a crib that we put up in the girls' room. Your Grandma would take care of you everyday so your Mama could go to work. It was fun to watch her play with you and feed you. And when you were old enough she had you help in the kitchen. She even made you your own little rolling pin from a broom handle, just your size, for making tortillas. She told me to sand it until it was 'baby smooth.'"

"I remember. I still have that rolling pin. And I remember trying so hard to make the tortillas round—I still can't make them as round as Grandma's. But you're getting us off track—what made you want to move to Riverside?"

4

Riverside, Oranges, Roses & Magdalena

"Boy, you're rushing me—are you hungry?"

"That chili is smelling like it's done. So..." I urged him to continue.

"Okay, okay. When I was about 50, we decided to move to Riverside because one time we had taken a drive out to see a friend of mine from work. We drove along Highway 91; it went through the hills and along the Santa Ana River. There were little stands along the way to stop at and get out of the car. We bought oranges and the coldest soda ever from the stand near Corona. When we got to Riverside, we were driving down Victoria Avenue. Your Grandma rolled down the window and took in a deep breath. She looked at me with excitement and said, 'Can you smell it? The sweet oranges and the roses mixed together—Oh, it's like heaven!' Plus, all the hills reminded her of Magdalena. There were little hills in town, but when you took a good look around, you could see the big mountains surrounding the Inland Empire. So, we saved up enough money to buy a brand new house. It was 1972, and they had just built a new track of homes right off of Van Buren Avenue. Your Grandma fell in love with it. It was the first 'new' house either of us had ever had. It was everything she wanted. There was a market nearby, the General Hospital not too far, and there was a brand new high school for your Aunt Bea to attend. She was going to be a senior—and she wasn't too happy about leaving her friends, but she liked the idea of a brand new house and having her very own room. There were also lots of grassy hills close by for you to climb. Plus, people kept horses right at the base of the hills. It kind of made you feel like you were out in the country, but you had everything you needed close by. And I know that no one else could see it, but your Grandma claimed that she could see 'The Lady of the Mountain' in the hills right by the house. She said she felt safe there—like she was being watched over by Mary Magdalene—just like in Magdalena."

"Wow! I didn't know that Riverside reminded Grandma of Magdalena. She never told me that."

"Well, in a way, Riverside and the surrounding mountains are a lot like Magdalena because there aren't too many places in the United States that have high mountains with snow in the middle of a desert. That's one thing Riverside and Magdalena have in common."

"That's true. One of my friends, a new girl, just moved here from Georgia—her daddy works at March Air Force Base—and she said she thought it was the weirdest thing that the only green spots in summer are the orange groves. She even told me that her Mama was afraid to move here because of all the little mountains popping up all over the place, and the big ones weren't far off—I guess she was just used to flat." It made me wonder if they studied Geography in Georgia.

"I think you are more like your Grandma than you realize. You love these hills and mountains as much as she did," Grandpa suggested.

"Well, I know I really loved playing in the hills. I'd spend all day up there—riding my green bike like it was a horse, and pretending to be a Cahuilla girl in the wild. I would come home so hungry from riding my bike all day. From around the corner I could smell

—even taste—Grandma's green chili, frijoles, and tortillas. Oh, I can still smell them."

"Uh, I think that's *our* chile you're smelling, miss."

"Okay, so it is," I admitted. "But I was kind of wishing..." I stopped--thinking like Grandpa did when he would tell me his story--about what to put in and what to leave out.

"What were you wishing?" Grandpa asked. "Were you wishing the same thing I was wishing?"

"I don't know. We're you wishing that Grandma was here with us?" I asked with a shaky voice.

"M'hunny, even though it's been almost a year, I wish that *all* the time. My heart aches every time I think of how young she was when she died. Only 47 years old. She suffered so much, but never let it show. I don't think I could ever be as brave. I will always love and miss your Grandma. But you know, I feel her with us all the time. And every time I look at you, I see your Grandma's smile and her kind eyes. You even have her coloring. She was fair with green eyes just like yours."

Grandpa brushed my cheek to wipe away the tears. I was remembering all the times I would ride my bike to General Hospital to sit with her while she was on the Dialysis machine. She always wanted me to read to her while the machine cleaned out her blood. I remember feeling scared, but I didn't want her to know--so I just read. Sometimes I read my favorite things like the little picture encyclopedias that she would buy for me at the grocery store. Other times I would read from the Highlights magazines that they had at the hospital. I loved learning from all those articles. As much as I didn't want my Grandma to be in the hospital, I did love those moments that we shared—just the two of us. She would always introduce me to the nurses, and tell them that I was her teacher, and that every time I read to her, she learned something new. Maybe that's why I love reading non-fiction so much. I felt so proud to be at my Grandma's side. When she finally died, I was so sad. I didn't know what I was going to do. She was such a big part of my life, and I didn't want to let go of her.

Grandpa could see I was lost in thought. "We better get back to the chile. Did you find out everything you needed for your project?" He asked trying to change the subject.

"Well that depends." I said.

"It depends on what?" Grandpa gave me a puzzled look. "I told you why we moved to California, and why we moved to Riverside—so what's left?"

"It depends on whether or not you are going to tell me the secret ingredient to making your chili. You know that no one can make it like you."

5

Always Make Chile
with Someone You Love

"Oh, so my secret is what you are after? Well, unfortunately all I can teach you today is how to make your own chile."

"What?" I asked in disbelief. "But we made your chili today."

"No Mija. *You* chopped the wood for the fire. *You* roasted the chiles. *You* even felt your hands burn while you peeled them. *You* stirred them into the pot and let them mix with all the other ingredients."

"But Grandpa," I interrupted "It was your story that you were telling."

"Yes. But you are part of my story and you added in your memories—your ingredients—So, this pot on the stove is filled with *your* chile. And now whenever you make it, you'll add in more memories—some might be happy and some might be sad, but they will be yours."

"But what if it doesn't taste like your chili?" I asked, feeling a little disappointed.

"Well, it probably won't—we all bring something new to the story—something new to the *olla*."

"So that means if I make the chili with someone else, it will taste different?"

"Of course, that's why you should always make chile with someone you love."

"Let's taste the chili, Grandpa. It's time," I insisted.

We both grabbed a spoon and carefully lifted the lid. A ribbon of steam laced with flavor snuck out from around the edges of the lid. We scooped up a little chili in our spoons, and I started to put it in my mouth.

"Wait!" Grandpa warned, "Let it cool. A burnt tongue cannot appreciate the layers of flavor and makes for bad memories."

"Oh, right," I said with an understanding nod. "I'll blow on it."

I started to blow a gentle stream of air over the chili and a delicate film formed on the top of the spoon. I wanted so badly to just put the whole spoonful in my watering mouth--all at once. But Grandpa's warning was still fresh in my mind, so I just barely let the tip of my lips touch the chili to feel if it was cool enough. Then I took a tiny bit into my mouth. The flavors swirled over my tongue and rose onto my palate. My eyes automatically closed as I took in all the layers of love and memories. The roasted chilies had suffered just enough—not too hot, but hot enough to remind me of the desert wind. The sharp garlic and onions had mellowed with time as they married with the chilies, stock, and seasonings to create a strong bond that could not be broken.

With eyes still closed, I let out a sigh, "Mmm, Yumm."

Grandpa gently patted me on the shoulder, "Great Chile, M'hunny. The flavors speak of you."

"I taste a few of your stories in here too, Grandpa. Thank you for teaching me and for helping me with my Social Studies project." I gave Grandpa a big hug.

"So, are we going to serve some frijoles and tortillas with this chile? Or are we just going to stand over the pot at the stove?" He asked.

"Well, I guess we should share with everyone else. How about if we put everything into big serving bowls on the table? That way people can serve as much as they want. Plus, they have to come and sit with us at the table." Since Grandma died, we didn't really set the table and eat together every night—I really missed that.

"I like that idea. That way we can see their faces when they taste your chile."

Just when we were finished putting everything on the table, my Mama, Aunts, Uncles, and little brother Sean came walking in.

"Smells like the chili is done," said my Uncle Julian as he put a few large scoops of chili on top of his frijoles.

Aunt Luella was right behind him with a tortilla already in her hand. "I want to see how hot it is before I put it on the plate—is it just right?" she asked, looking at me with a smile.

"Mmmm. ¡Qué Sabroso!" said my Mama. "You can make chile for me anytime you want, Mija."

"Me too, Sister!" Sean smiled at me with his mouth full.

"Thanks Mama, but Grandpa helped a lot," I said looking at Grandpa.

He smiled at me with a mouthful of chili and gave me a wink.

"Well, you sure can tell that you made your chili with someone you love," said my Aunt Bea.

I felt so proud of my chili. I finally learned how to make Grandpa's New Mexico Green Chili--with my California twist. We all sat around the table in the kitchen, eating chili, smiling, laughing, and talking about memories. I sat there, hypnotized by the moment, and it struck me—*I had brought everyone back to the table.*

"You know, I think you should add the chile recipe to your project board," Grandpa suggested.

"But I was just supposed to tell why our family came to California," I replied.

"Well everybody will be telling that, and most everyone's project will tell about coming to California to make a better life for their families. Some of your classmates may even focus on how hard it was and what they had to give up to come here. But you can tell them what we brought to California. We brought our tradition of making chile—you are the one who needs to pass that on now."

And with that, Grandpa handed me a piece of paper—old and stained with the juice of roasted chilies.

"Here, this belongs to you now. It's the official Nuñez Chile Recipe—It says so on the top of the page. See? It has your great Grandfather's name on it, Severo Nuñez."

I unfolded the paper being careful not to rip it. To me, it was like some sacred document that contained the secret of life. I took Grandpa's challenge to heart. I knew I must pass on the tradition—I must not forget. So now I pass it on to you—so *you* won't forget.

Nuñez Family Green Chili Recipe
(Always cook with adult supervision)

Ingredients:

- 6 to 8 New Mexico Green Chilies *(fire-roasted, peeled, seeded, and chopped)*
- 2 cloves garlic *(crushed)*
- Beef *(any cut will do, but the better the quality the better the taste—cut into bite-size pieces)*
- Fresh oregano *(dried is fine, but you get more flavor from fresh)*
- 2 or 3 tomatoes *(fire-roasted with the chilies, peeled, chopped)*
- 1 large brown or white onion *(fire-roasted, peeled, chopped)*
- 1 tablespoon flour
- 1 ½ to 2 cups of beef stock
- Salt and seasonings *(optional but good: cumin, coriander, and cinnamon, to taste)*

Directions:

Roast your chilies on the barbeque grill, turning them as the skin gets blistered. When all the chilies (and other vegetables) are roasted, put them in an airtight container to cool. When they are cool enough to handle, put on clean kitchen gloves (or your hands will burn!) and peel the skin off the chilies. If you like a milder chili, you may want to remove the seeds too. Chop them and set them aside.

In a heavy cast-iron skillet, put a little oil (just enough to cover the bottom). When the pan is hot, add the meat and brown it. Sprinkle flour over the meat to coat it. When the meat is evenly browned, remove it and set aside for later. Add in chilies, onion, garlic, and tomatoes. When the juices from the vegetables seep out and the onions have become slightly brown, lightly coat with flour. Let it brown up a bit more and add the beef stock. Return the meat to the pot. Season, and bring to a boil. Immediately, turn the flame down low and let the chili simmer until the meat is done to your liking and the broth has thickened up. With a spoon, scoop out some chili. Let the chili cool a little before you try it—"a burnt tongue cannot appreciate the layers of flavor and makes bad memories." Adjust seasonings as you like—don't forget to stir in your good memories and love.

Enjoy!

Epilogue

While investigating my family's heritage and trying to discover the secret ingredients to my Grandpa Julian's New Mexico Green Chili, I came upon a realization-- It often changes depending on who is listening. As with any oral tradition, changes to the recipes (and stories) take place. When I asked my Grandpa about his life he recounted highlights that he thought were important and then related them to mine.

Looking back on Grandpa's story I realize there is so much more to our family's heritage. In all, my grandfather (Julian Romero Nuñez) has ten grandchildren, including my brother and eight other cousins. At last count, Julian has fourteen great-grandchildren—and I'm sure more to follow. How different were the stories he told to them? Or am I the only one who has asked? On my ancestral quest, I found that my second cousin, Severo (Sevy), had already done a lot of research about our family. He found that:

> "It is likely that Nuñes was the earliest name, a name in the registry of Sephardic Jews who were expelled from Spain/Portugal by the Spanish King and Queen, Ferdinand and Isabella..." Records were also found that suggest, "The earliest

Nuñez in the New World may have been a soldier sent to the most remote northern outpost of New Spain, the presidio of San Elizario, located a few miles from present day El Paso, Texas. Here we have located records of our family Juan Jose Nuñez married to Vicenta Marquez with a son nicknamed "Santos" short for Santa Cruz who later became the father of Severo Nuñez..." Severo later married Maria Eugenia Alvarez (grandmother of Julian Nuñez—my grandfather).

I'm convinced that if Grandpa Julian were telling the story to another person he would choose different events. The same can be said for passing on family traditions. The basic recipe for Nuñez Family Green Chili is the same, but feel free to add ingredients (and memories) of your own. Thank you Cousin, for helping me gather a few more pieces to our family's puzzling heritage. Thank you Grandpa, for sharing your life with me—and your recipe.

Glossary

Ajo (ah-hoe) garlic

Calabasita (call-a-ba-seata) summer squash, like zucchini

Cebolla (se-boy-ya) onion

Carne (car-nay) meat

Frijoles (free-hole-es) slow cooked beans (usually pinto beans).

Míja (Me-ha) short for Mí Híja which means my daughter or my girl. Also used as an endearment for little girls with whom you are very familiar.

Olla (Oi-ya) big cooking pot (sometimes ceramic or cast iron)

Pepino (pep-ee-no) cucumber

Tortilla (Tore-tee-ya) flat rolled out bread usually made of flour or corn and cooked on a hot flat griddle called a **comal (Coe-mal)**.

¿Qué No? (Kay-no) an expression loosely translated to mean "you think?" Use when you are asking someone if they agree with you.

¡Qué Sabroso! (Kay Sab-ro-zo) an expression used after eating something that you think is very tasty, savory, and flavorful.

Rancho (ran-cho) Large pieces of land that were given to ranchers by Spain with the understanding that they (ranchers) would live on and improve the land by farming and raising livestock.

CCC Civilian Conservation Corps was a public works program that provided jobs for unskilled young men during the Great Depression. It was part of the New Deal implemented by President Roosevelt. (1933-1942).

The Great Depression The Great Depression was a time of economic hardship. It started in about 1929 and lasted until the late 1930s or early 1940s. It was very hard for people to find work and many people were left homeless.

WWII (World War Two) was a global war that lasted from 1939 to 1945. Most of the world's nations were involved, including the great powers like the United States and Russia. They were organized into two opposing military alliances: the Allies and the Axis. It was the most widespread war in history, with more than 100 million military men and women.

USO (United States Organization) During World War II, the USO became the G. I.'s "home away from home" and provided entertainment to the troops. Almost 1.5 million Americans volunteered their services in some way.

Nuñez Family Album

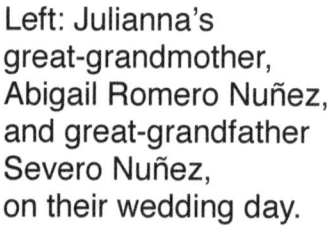

Left: Julianna's great-grandmother, Abigail Romero Nuñez, and great-grandfather Severo Nuñez, on their wedding day.

Right: Great-grandfather Severo Nuñez, with Grandpa Julian as a young child.

Left: Grandpa Julian and Grandma Martha.

Left: Julianna's Grandpa Julian and Grandma Martha on their wedding day.

Right: Grandpa Julian, Grandma Martha, and Julianna's mother, Magdalena.

Above: Grandpa Julian, Grandma Martha, Julianna's mom, Magdalena, and Julianna's Uncle Julian, on vacation from California to Magdalena, New Mexico.

Right:
Julianna Maya Cruz,
9 months old

Left: Julianna with her mother, Magdalena.

Above: Julianna and brother Sean
in Riverside, California

Julianna then...

...and now: Third row from front, second from left:
Julianna Maya Cruz
Second row from front, seated in the center:
Grandpa Julian, on his 80th birthday

Above: Magdalena, New Mexico, 1950
Below: Riverside, California, 2011

About Julianna Maya Cruz

Julianna Maya Cruz is an elementary teacher and writer from Riverside, CA. She has been teaching for 14 years and is the author of *The Tale of Tommy & Teresa Trout: A Learning Journey from Egg to Fry* and *Two Chilies*. Julianna is currently a member of The Inlandia Institute's Advisory Council and Publications Committee. With the help of The Inlandia Institute, Julianna developed and taught Children's Creative Writing Workshops that have produced chapbooks of student work.

Other Inlandia Publications

INLANDIA ELECTRONIC PUBLICATIONS

Inlandia: A Literary Journey, an on-line journal
Edited by Cati Porter

Audio Guide
Inlandia: A Literary Journey Through California's Inland Empire
Moderated by Gayle Brandeis

OTHER INLANDIA IMPRINT PUBLICATIONS

Two Chilies/Dos Chiles
Julianna Cruz

2011 Writing from Inlandia
Editorial Board

INLANDIA IMPRINT BOOKS FROM HEYDAY

Backyard Birds of the Inland Empire
Sheila N. Kee

Dream Street
Douglas F. McCulloh,
forward by D.J. Waldie

Inlandia:A Literary Journey Through California's Inland Empire
Edited by Gayle Wattawa, introduction by Susan Straight

No Place for a Puritan: The Literature of California's Deserts
Edited by Ruth Nolan

Expected in March 2012
Rose Hill
Carlos Cortez

About the Inlandia Institute

The Inlandia Institute is a regional non-profit literary center. We seek to bring focus to the richness of the literary enterprise that has existed in this region for ages. The mission of the Inlandia Institute is to recognize, support and expand literary activity in all of its forms through community programs in the Inland Empire, thereby deepening people's awareness, understanding, and appreciation of this unique, complex, and creatively vibrant region.

The Institute publishes high quality regional writing in print and electronic form including books published in partnership with Heyday under the Inlandia Institute imprint as well as: *Writing From Inlandia: Work of the Inlandia Creative Writing Workshops*; the online literary journal, *Inlandia: A Literary Journey; and*, starting in 2012, books directly under the Inlandia imprint, including *Two Chilies/Dos Chiles*, a children's chapter book by Julianna Cruz.

Inlandia presents free public literary programming featuring authors who live in, work in, and/or write about Inland Southern California. We also provide Creative Literacy Programs for children and youth and hold creative writing workshops for teens and adults.

To learn more about the Inlandia Institute please visit our website at InlandiaInstitute.org.